Winning
with
Whiskers™

*A Business Fable
about Overcoming Barriers
by Knowing Yourself and Others*

Winning with Whiskers™

*A Business Fable
about Overcoming Barriers
by Knowing Yourself and Others*

Dawn F. Landry

Dedication

This book is dedicated to the many technical professional colleagues and friends I have had the pleasure to work alongside throughout my rich and rewarding career.

You have taught me so much, and I carry those lessons into this book, as well as Authentizity's consulting and training practice.

Contents

Part Three: Extra Whiskers Exploration

Appendix

Preface

I have had a front-row seat to see the achievements and challenges of technical professionals in their relationship advancement responsibilities, especially concerning clients and business development. I have heard the rumblings of my colleagues and peers about how they do not want to sell, do not like salespeople, did not go to school to be a salesperson, and a myriad of other objections.

However, I have also witnessed firsthand that when these same technicians discover and own their relationship-building styles, they engineer the foundation for a future that impacts their career trajectory and beyond.

In a world filled with lots of interesting characters, what better way to relay a story about how we all have unique hardwiring that we use to create, cultivate, and deepen long-lasting relationships than a fable with a giraffe, robot, entertaining sea lion, workhorse, and old dog?

Of note, each character (yes, even the robot) has whiskers.

Animals use their whiskers for sensory functions, spatial awareness, hunting and foraging, communication, balance, and orientation.

Robots use their whiskers for environmental sensing, measurement and precision, exploration, research, and enhanced autonomy.

In humans, our whiskers are not as obvious, but they are as beneficial. Our whiskers are our experiences, education, culture, diversity, and so much more. They are special to each individual, regardless of type or use.

With knowledge, self-awareness, and practice, all whiskers are integral in advancing us and our future business relationship successes.

As this tale will tell, *we all have whiskers, and we can all win with our special whiskers!*

Get The Most From This Fable Experience

The best way to consume this book is to read the fable first and then explore the character profiles. The latter part of the book contains an exercise with multiple questions. These questions are designed to help you identify/overcome any barriers, and begin the discovery of your unique, winning whiskers.

Part One

The Fable

Chapter One

A Technical Business Scenario

One regular business day in a steady but non-eventful economic season, GiGi, the giraffe, decided to expand her company's roster of consultants.

She and her assistant, Willie, the wise owl, researched firms and called industry-trusted advisors for insight and referrals before narrowing the field to four possible firms.

GiGi then asked Willie to invite all the candidates to a group briefing about the new business opportunity.

Harlie, a seasoned workhorse, arrived early. He sat inside the lobby, exuding confidence as someone who had seen and experienced it all.

Next to Harlie, with nervous energy on the edge of his seat yet equipped with all his state-of-the-art gadgets, was Rockie, the robot. His sleek metal exterior shimmered under the bright, fluorescent office lighting as he distracted himself with his wrist-activated AI assistant. The device was his go-to solution to avoid engaging in conversation.

Dannie, the old dog, arrived next. Quiet and observant but approachable, Dannie did not take a seat at first but chose to strike up a conversation with Willie, who had already greeted each of the candidates.

Willie invited them into the main conference room at the designated time.

Running late from a previous meeting, Stevie, the entertaining sea lion, bolted in, breathlessly apologizing and explaining her tardiness. She was very animated, with a twinkle in her eye and a sense of humor to match. The group in the conference room erupted in laughter at Stevie's hilarious description of her morning escapades.

GiGi was already in the conference room and began the meeting by expressing appreciation for each firm's interest. She walked them through a presentation, explaining her company's history and technical service offerings. She then shared her expectations when hiring future consultants and defined the initial scope of work for their services.

She relayed her company's commitment to partnering with consultants, as proven by its fair contract and payment terms. Professional yet cordial and communicative, GiGi demonstrated to the group that she would not waste their time and would value their contributions to her company.

She advised them that the next steps would include one-on-one consultant briefings with each of them so that they could define, "Why you? Why not them? What's your firm's value proposition and differentiator?"

In closing, GiGi asked Willie to schedule meetings with each candidate as she thanked them again for their interest. GiGi then excused herself and left to prepare for her next meeting. It was another bumper-to-bumper day.

Harlie and Rockie did not hang around. They immediately left after Willie coordinated their respective follow-up briefings.

Dannie stayed a little longer to ensure she did not miss any nuance of the pickup conversations or the company's general environment.

However, Stevie lingered even longer since her lunch meeting was in the area. Ever charming, she chatted Willie up and even met other team members of GiGi's company who happened to walk past the lobby.

Chapter Two

The Individual Firm Briefings and Their Follow-Up with GiGi

H ere is what happened
in their follow up,
one-on-one firm briefings
with GiGi:

Rockie, the Robot

Rockie met with GiGi first. He reluctantly went in but did not want to be there because he did not consider himself a salesperson or good at sales. The only thing that settled his nerves was his computer—it was his shield.

Despite all this, he came fully equipped as always, having extensively researched GiGi's company. He prepared a pitch centered around his firm and how he would maximize innovation to deliver measurable results for GiGi. Rockie stated that he was hardwired to do this.

To demonstrate his efficiency, he completed his presentation well before the allotted time was over. Rockie did not follow up with GiGi after the meeting because he did not want her to feel like he was a pest bothering her.

Stevie, the Entertaining Sea Lion

Next, Stevie was up. She greeted GiGi with a quick joke to break the ice. Stevie then proceeded to talk boisterously about how she loved GiGi's company. In her monologue, Stevie made many predictions about GiGi and her company's needs.

She then talked about last night's big event in town and invited GiGi to join them at Stevie's firm's suite for the next one. GiGi barely got a word in edgewise, and then their time was up.

Before leaving the building, Stevie connected with Willie to get that next event on GiGi's calendar.

Harlie, the Workhorse

Harlie was next. Like Rockie, Harlie does not consider himself salesy because he especially does not want to be known as slick. It all seems too slimy for him. However, once he was there, Harlie instantly clicked with GiGi, asking her about her business and its needs and paralleling this to his firm's successes.

He correlated how his firm could add value to GiGi's company. He later followed up through Willie to offer GiGi a company tour of his facilities to demonstrate firsthand what they had discussed.

Once back at his office, Harlie reported on the briefing to his colleagues. He confidently told them that he could talk about their firm and its services so easily because he believes in what they do, as evidenced by all their repeat business.

Dannie, the Old Dog

Lastly, Dannie took a completely different approach during her company briefing. She sat down, looked into GiGi's eyes, and then asked GiGi what matters most to her.

Ever present, she took the time to listen to GiGi's every word and then took her cues as GiGi led the conversation. Dannie later returned to her office and customized a program to GiGi's identified needs.

Within 24 hours, Dannie delivered the program draft to GiGi's inbox with recommended dates for a follow-up discussion. Dannie copied Willie on the email to ensure that calendar coordination was as easy as possible for GiGi.

Chapter Three

So, Who Got the Deal?

Who did GiGi select?

Well, it depends...

It depends on who GiGi is, her unique characteristics, and the type of person she responds to when cultivating and advancing relationships.

A Client Debrief with GiGi / Dissecting the Deal

How could these very different relationship cultivation and advancement approaches yield a similar, positive client win?

The answer lies in who GiGi is and what her drivers are for a successful new consultant solution. In a post-interview debrief with GiGi, she shared insights into her motivations for each decision.

Why GiGi chose:

Rockie, the Robot

Rockie was extremely analytical and efficient with GiGi and her time. GiGi appreciated this because her time is in demand.

He thoroughly went through all his firm's features and benefits. GiGi was impressed by how she could lean on Rockie for research about his firm, the industry, and the trends he predicted for the future.

GiGi considers herself cutting-edge and an early adopter. When Rockie demonstrated to her that his firm's services offered GiGi's company a way that she could use innovative technologies as real-world solutions to have an edge over her competition, it was an easy decision for her.

Stevie, the Entertaining Sea Lion

Stevie is quite a people person and a lot of fun. She is also funny, but not in an inappropriate way. She made GiGi laugh and helped her relax while they were talking business.

GiGi shares that joie de vivre philosophy and knows no stranger herself. GiGi enjoyed her interaction with Stevie so much that she took Stevie up on her offer to accompany her to the next big event in town. Their working friendship further developed and has now translated into sales for Stevie's firm.

Harlie, the Workhorse

Harlie never makes promises he cannot keep. As the years have gone by, his reputation for reliability has spread like wildfire. If you wanted the best, you went to Harlie. That is how GiGi even had Harlie's name on her list of potential candidates.

Unlike his competition (Rockie, who utilized geofencing to purchase ad space in areas that GiGi trafficked selectively, and Stevie, who was ever present on social media with lots of posts about her business activities), Harlie had a plethora of great referrals and repeat clients which had sustained his firm for several decades.

This deep experience and repeat business gave GiGi great confidence in her decision to go with Harlie's firm.

GiGi is risk-averse when making decisions. She also really liked that Harlie took the time to offer her a follow-up demonstration of his service offerings at his firm's location. It sealed the deal!

Dannie, the Old Dog

Cultivating connections is the key to Dannie's success. That goes beyond knowing her clients by name. She understands their needs deeply and tailors her service offerings to match them.

For GiGi, trust is everything. She individualizes her clients' experiences, so she detests boilerplate solutions. Selecting Dannie's firm was easy because Dannie looked GiGi in the eye, genuinely listened to her, and promptly delivered a customized solution to fit GiGi's needs.

Consideration / Call to Action

As different as they are, all the candidates have one common denominator.

What is that similarity?

They each possess their own unique type of whiskers, and most importantly, they own them. That way, they can authentically represent themselves to connect with GiGi, cultivating and advancing their relationship to ultimately win the contract with their whiskers.

Even the most technically hardwired candidates, like Rockie and Harlie, were able to succeed. Winning proved to each of them that even though they disassociate any idea of themselves as salespeople, they can still influence and persuade a decision in their favor. That is all that sales is, by the way. Sales is influencing a decision in your favor!

As you consider this business fable, one challenge is:

Do you recognize your uniqueness and value in the whiskers you bring to your clients, within your firm, and most importantly, to yourself? If you don't, then how might you begin to?

Here is a call to action:

What three relationship cultivation and advancement tactics will you deploy in the next 30 days that are unique to you?

Chapter Four

The Moral of the Story

We can create relationships and influence decisions based on our innate hardwiring and by knowing our whiskers. To do this successfully, we must possess self-awareness to discover our uniqueness and how it corresponds (and hopefully connects) to the person across the table from us.

It also mandates that we know our clients as individuals and understand that they are as different as we are. We sometimes must adapt our approach to their needs.

A smidge of Rockie's analysis and a splash of Stevie's jovial congeniality, mixed with Harlie's authenticity and hands-on demonstration, topped with Dannie's ability to stay present and make every client feel seen, goes a long way in cultivating, advancing, and then retaining client relationships.

You see, the foundation of successful business relationships lies not only in the technology and tools we wield or the great times we offer but also in the genuine connections we forge.

We must listen, adapt, and serve our clients with the utmost dedication.

Envision yourself here.
What are your whiskers?

Chapter Five

Winning with Whiskers™ Takeaway Summary

If I were to sum up all of the things that I've learned from three decades in business, it would culminate into this simple, seven-word phrase:

Without Business Relationships, You Have No Business.

To succeed in business relationship cultivation and advancement, you must:

1. Know yourself and appreciate your whiskers.

2. Identify and explore your relationship
   connection type.

3. You won't connect with everyone and that is okay. They are not your people. You have to find your people. They are out there.

4. Stay present and be a great listener.

5. Always be on the lookout for something to follow up on with someone.

And, most importantly, you must:

Get to the relationship before you get to the ask!

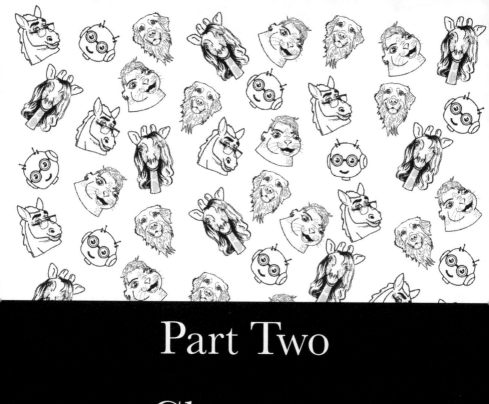

Part Two

Character Profiles

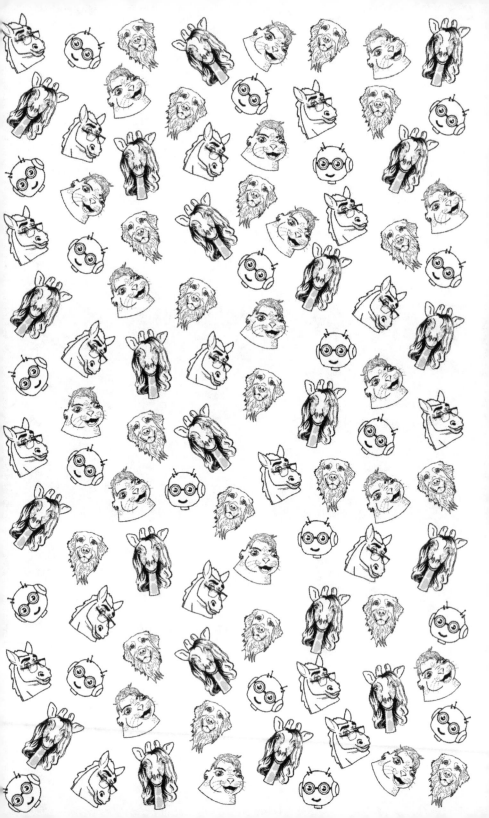

Chapter Six

About Rockie

Rockie's Early Relationship Capabilities

Engineered is a perfect word to describe Rockie. He is hardwired to analyze and learn new concepts to provide insight and knowledge to his clients. By deploying the latest trends and technologies, his clients stay on the cutting edge of the industry.

One of Rockie's greatest abilities is leveraging what some of his competition may view as toys to improve the effectiveness and efficiency of his clients' work. He naturally sees the positive outcomes of employing new technologies and can skillfully articulate the benefits of early adoption.

Rockie's whiskers are especially unique, providing antennae-like sensors with deliberate and consistent output for his clients.

However, Rockie struggles most with networking events and anything he views as cold calling, whether it is actual cold calling or not. His formula for success is finding like-minded people with whom he can share the data and statistics that back up his firm's technologies.

Rockie's Early Relationship Preparation

Rockie is methodical and detail-oriented in his preparation for meetings. He always has an agenda and leverages research and technology to get his point across. This strategy also applies to how he approaches early business development. He utilizes tools such as social media (specifically LinkedIn), his firm's website, SEO placement, geofencing, and artificial intelligence to drive traffic and awareness to his firm and its service offerings.

Rockie's Follow-Up (Long-Term)

Rockie prefers to download all his knowledge and experience with his clients and prospects when he meets with them, so there is no question about his abilities. With that said, he waits for them to contact him as a follow-up, as he never wants to seem pushy or too anxious to a potential client.

A Special Rockie Tip

Rockie works at warp speed and is a natural-born learner. His consumption and absorption of information amaze his clients and colleagues alike. However, Rockie's blind spot is being unaware that not everyone processes in the same manner as he does. Bite-sized chunks are sometimes more easily digested over time.

Rather than coming across as robotic and formulaic, Rockie is at his best when he can get out from behind the data (and his computer, which acts as his shield). Stretching himself this way allows others to get to know him and vice versa.

Information/data is power, but humans are unique and nuanced. We cannot be synthesized into categories without the curiosity and time required to get to know and go deeper into the relationships without assumptions, generalizations, or stereotyping.

Chapter Seven

About Stevie

Stevie's Early Relationship Capabilities

Stevie is bold and confident. Her positive energy and laughter are infectious. Because of this, Stevie never meets a stranger and is never at a loss for words.

The firm Stevie represents hired her to be its brand ambassador throughout the business community. Stevie is naturally charming and always the life of the party. She enjoys being out in the market, networking, and hosting clients and allies for various events that her firm sponsors.

Stevie knows how to coordinate the best and most fun activities. For her, the more the merrier.

However, when she has limited capacity, she also knows how to strategically develop her invitation list to maximize the experience and investment with the best possible mix of people in the group.

Stevie's Early Relationship Preparation

Early in her career, Stevie's mentor shared with her, "There are sniffers, and then there are closers related to these kinds of service sales."

Stevie considers herself a great sniffer. It's part of her unique whiskers.

Stevie's relationships open doors because she is a master connector. Her network is always at work for her.

Through her connections, Stevie is in the know about everything happening in the city in its early, formative stages. She leverages this intel for introductions to decision-makers like GiGi.

She then partners with technical professionals in her firm to advance and transition her relationships to them. They then negotiate and close the deal.

Stevie's Follow-Up (Long-Term)

While she considers the internal client relationship management (CRM) documentation and reporting monotonous, she leverages her assistant and artificial intelligence technology to allow her to spend time doing what she loves most—being in front of people.

Other than that, Stevie considers her follow-up to be more organic and spontaneous. By attending so many outreach outings throughout any given week or month, her theory is that she is bound to run into the people she needs to see at some point.

A Special Stevie Tip

Stevie's ease of conversation is a great attribute, especially at networking events. However, her blind spot is knowing when to stop talking and listen to understand the client's needs.

Through the years, Stevie has learned how to read her audience. Thus, she knows when her chattiness is getting annoying to the person on the other side of the table.

She has also adapted this to her written style. For some of her clients, she understands how to provide just the facts in bulleted form. If they have questions, then they will ask for more.

Chapter Eight

About Harlie

Harlie's Early Relationship Capabilities

As a workhorse with unique whiskers, Harlie knows the importance of planting, sowing, and harvesting in their due seasons. He sees the parallels in how these cycles apply to relationships and understands that relationship cultivation and advancement are marathons and never sprints.

A man of few words, Harlie typically speaks last in a meeting, but his words are deliberate and authentically originate from his desire to serve. Also, Harlie has never made promises he could not keep.

Harlie's Early Relationship Preparation

Like Dannie, Harlie's repeat business is the envy of his competition.

As Harlie's reputation grew over the years, word spread like wildfire. If you wanted the best, you went to Harlie. That is how GiGi even had Harlie's name for her list of considerations.

Once Harlie works for a client, repeat business is easy. Known far and wide for his reputation and consistent delivery, he has built his business on the 80/20 rule — 80%+ of his business comes from 20% of his repeat clients.

Harlie sees no need to advertise, use social media, or even heavily entertain his clients. Word of mouth is his best friend and business development tool.

Harlie's Follow-Up (Long-Term)

Harlie believes that the proof is in the pudding. He walks into each new client meeting knowing he will offer a tour of his company at some point, whether in the initial conversation or as part of his follow-up.

He is very proud of his colleagues and their repeatable, reliable services to their clients, so it is easy for him to want to demonstrate his firm's capabilities in this manner.

Harlie gets new business by exhibiting his firm's services through company site visits, personnel introductions, etc. This approach is natural for him and does not come off as bragging.

The "product sells itself" is his philosophy and belief.

A Special Harlie Tip

Harlie's biggest watch out is that while he can quickly adapt lessons learned into his firm's best practices, he typically is not an early adopter of new ideas.

In fact, he is reticent to change with technology and innovation. Harlie has a strong inner critic, so he wants proven evidence that a change is necessary before he considers it. He lives by the mantra, "If it's not broken, why fix it?"

Harlie's skepticism may make his firm and their services obsolete unless they can adapt and flex to the market's needs.

Chapter Nine

About Dannie

Dannie's Early Relationship Capabilities

Dannie likes people, plain and simple. However, she prefers one-on-one conversations to those in large crowds. (It is a definite quality over quantity for her.)

Dannie believes that you have your friends, and then you have *your friends*. Special *friends* are in the inner sanctum. They gained trust and credibility with Dannie long ago, and she is loyal to them.

It is reciprocal, especially in her relationship cultivation and advancement style.

Nothing makes Dannie happier than truly getting to understand and know someone. That way, no assumptions are made. It is in her unique whiskers to establish trust and credibility.

Dannie's philosophy is that when someone hires her, they are saying, "Here is my career. Don't screw it up!"

The size of the deal—a few hundred or several million dollars—or where the money comes from —the individual's back pocket or the organization they work for—does not matter. Dannie believes that clients will only hire us if they look at us eyeball-to-eyeball and know we understand their needs.

Dannie has built strong relationships with her long-term clients, and they leverage her as a trusted advisor on a wide array of topics.

Dannie credits all her successes to being innately curious about lots of subjects. Most of all, Dannie is curious about people and their needs. She sees each person as an individual and makes no assumptions about them.

She is known far and wide for asking great questions. This gift of curiosity translates to Dannie's client meetings as she listens intently, throttles back, and lobs another insightful question over the table.

In doing so, she deepens her relationships by being a problem-finder *and* a problem-solver.

Dannie's Early Relationship Preparation

In advance of any new client introductions, Dannie best prepares herself by asking her close contacts for their insights about the person/firm she will meet.

Dannie's new business opportunities rarely come as cold calls. Like Harlie, Dannie prides herself on having repeat business relationships with clients who easily and readily refer new opportunities to Dannie.

When this happens, Dannie leans heavily on the perspectives those referrals provide about the synergies between the new client and Dannie's service offerings. She then prepares for the introduction accordingly.

Dannie is not a hard sell or pressure-driven person. She firmly believes it will work out if it is a good fit. Otherwise, the deal was never hers.

Her philosophy is that losses are okay. They just were not meant to be.

Dannie's Follow-Up (Long-Term)

Dannie is in it for the long haul. As mentioned previously, she values quality over quantity in relationships.

Professionally, that translates because her work relationships then become her friends. It is easy for her to stay in touch because she is genuinely interested in the lives of her connections.

Especially as it relates to clients, they love Dannie because they know she is not contacting them to take something from them.

She is there to give. (By the way, this is especially important during down market cycles when a client may not have any work for Dannie. Clients make note of Dannie being there in the good times and bad. It makes a difference to them to know which consultants only keep in touch when they have work to dish out.)

A Special Dannie Tip

Dannie is known for staying in touch. One of her most successful ways to stay in touch is periodically sending a "You are on my mind" email or text message to the people who matter most to her.

This simple gesture has an amazing impact because it deepens and elongates her relationships over time.

Additionally, Dannie continues to hone her communication capabilities. She tunes her ears to pick up on the nuggets that the person she is listening to is dropping. Dannie developed this talent, much like learning a new language. She gets better with time and experience, proactively developing this muscle.

In summary, Dannie's relationships are not transactional. They are fully in service and relational to the individual.

Part Three

Extra Whiskers Exploration

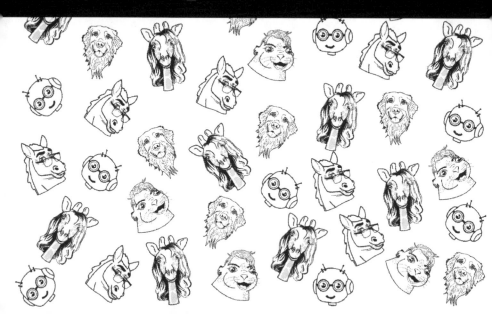

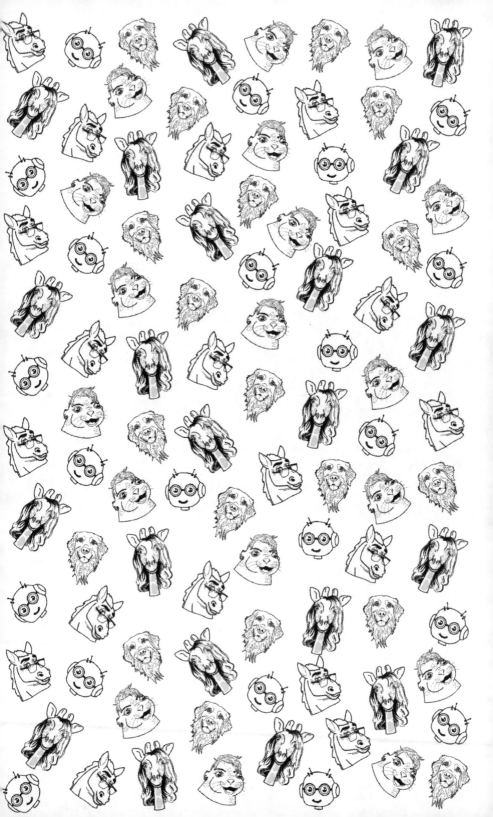

Stevie   **Harlie**   **GiGi**   **Dannie**   **Rockie**

Winning with Whiskers™ Exercise

◎ What was your overall take away from the fable?

_____

_____

_____

_____

_____

_____

_____

_____

_____

_____

_____

Stevie   **Harlie**   **GiGi**   **Dannie**   **Rockie**

Winning with Whiskers™ Exercise

◎ Which character was most like you? Share
your thoughts about this.

_____

_____

_____

_____

_____

_____

_____

_____

_____

_____

Stevie   Harlie   GiGi   Dannie   Rockie

Winning with Whiskers™ Exercise

◎ Which character was least like you? Share
your thoughts about this.

_____

_____

_____

_____

_____

_____

_____

_____

_____

_____

Stevie   Harlie   GiGi   Dannie   Rockie

Winning with Whiskers™ Exercise

◎ What three considerations/areas of
    opportunities do you now have about your
    own whiskers for your future?

_____

_____

_____

◎ From those three considerations/areas of
    opportunities, what three tactical activities
    will you commit to cultivate and advance
    your client relationships in the next 30 days?

_____

_____

_____

_____

Stevie   **Harlie**   **GiGi**   **Dannie**   **Rockie**

Winning with Whiskers™ Exercise

◎ Where might you hold yourself back?

_____

_____

_____

_____

_____

◎ What are you going to do about it?

_____

_____

_____

_____

_____

Appendix

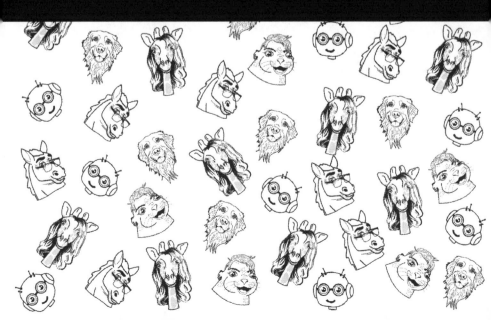

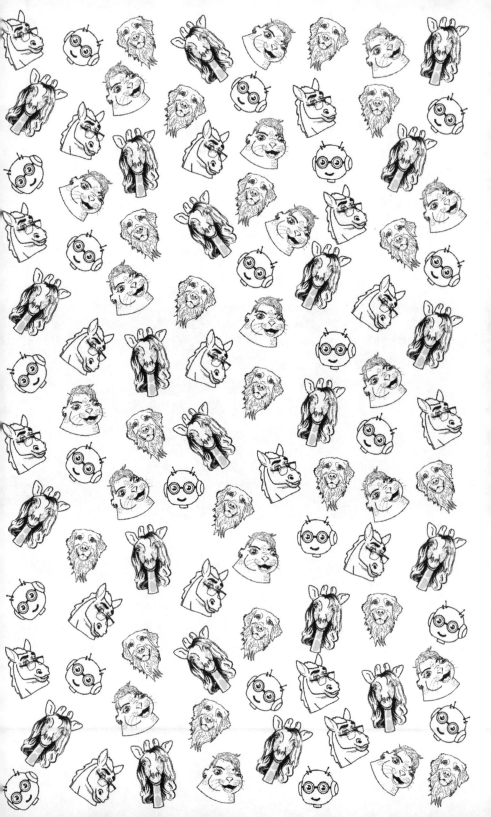

Acknowledgments

I am a collector—a collector of stories, information, and of people. Winning with Whiskers™ would not be possible without the experiences I have had and the expertise I have garnered from my big, bold, beautiful career. However, it would also not have been possible without the contributions of many whom I cherish dearly. I can't name them all, but I want to acknowledge a few.

To Rana Severs, you are right yet again. We were meant to know one another. Ever since that initial introduction so many years ago, we just clicked. I am so happy to call you a friend and ally. I am so thankful you are always there to translate my dreams into reality.

To Alyssa Curry, thank you for sharing your creativity with me. You made these characters come to life. They are now as real to others as they are to me in my imagination.

To my mentor and one of the greatest relationship cultivators I know, Dudley Van Ness. You coined the phrase *sniffers and closers*, and I give you full acknowledgment. Thank you. Most of all, thank you for investing in me as you did for many others and our futures.

To my greatest source of encouragement and support, Daran Landry. You inspire me every day. I am a better person because of you and our life's journey together.

Most of all, I give all glory and honor to God. Thank you for all the opportunities and for my special whiskers.

About the Author

Dawn F. Landry is a bestselling author, and an award-winning and nationally respected business professional.

Landry has spent more than half of her 31-year career in the corporate real estate industry, excelling in business development and marketing leadership positions within Houston's largest economic development organization, as well as international commercial construction companies. She works hand in glove with technical and operations team members to expand sales revenue.

In February 2017, she founded Authentizity, LLC, as an independent B2B growth strategist and a Gallup-Certified CliftonStrengths® Coach to provide consulting, training, and coaching services that optimize technical teams' engagement and productivity.

Landry also created *BD Dynamics, Empowering the Technical Minded,* a training program which advances the accountability, intentionality, and measurability of technical professionals' competencies within their relationship cultivation and advancement processes.

For more information, please visit:

» www.dawnflandry.com and www.authentizity. com

» LinkedIn: https://www.linkedin.com/in/dawn-f-landry/

Explore Other Books by Dawn F. Landry

Check out other books by Dawn F. Landry by visiting and following her Amazon Author page at https://www.amazon.com/author/dawnflandry.

Winning with Whiskers™ Consulting

Winning with Whiskers™ is a part of Authentizity's *BD Dynamics' Program*.

The fable is utilized for participants to readily envision their roles in cultivating and advancing their client relationships. That way, they can connect, no matter which character they identify with most.

In this training, participants work through a series of exercises to "own" their individual client approach, outreach, and maintenance style.

This fun and inspiring story helps even the most technically-minded service provider to expand their typical perceptions about business and client development so that they can overcome any self-limiting challenges.

Winning with Whiskers™ is the first book in the Winning with Whiskers™ series by Dawn F. Landry. Join us as our characters, Rockie, Harlie, Stevie, and Dannie, experience real-world business scenarios with their client, GiGi. In their individual journeys, they will be called upon to develop and advance new relationships, leveraging their unique whiskers to win work for their firms.

Stay tuned for the next book!